How to Bake the Best Delicious Fudge For All Seasons - In Your Kitchen

Kim Lambert and Charly Leetham

KIM LAMBERT and CHARLY LEETHAM

Dreamstone Publishing © 2014

www.dreamstonepublishing.com

Copyright © 2014 Kim Lambert and Charly Leetham

All rights reserved.

No parts of this work may be copied without the authors permission.

ISBN-13: 978-1-925499-62-9

Disclaimer

All cooking is an experiment in a sense, and many people come to the same or similar recipe over time. All recipes in this book have been derived from the author's personal experience, and that of friends and relatives. Should any bear a close resemblance to those used elsewhere, that is purely coincidental.

© Kim Lambert and Charly Leetham 2014, all rights reserved.

No parts of this work may be copied without the author's permission.

If you would like to provide feedback on this book please send it to info@dreamstonepublishing.com

Other Books in the "How to Bake the Best ....." Series

How to Bake the Best Delicious Valentine's Day Cupcakes - In Your Kitchen

By Kim Lambert

How to Bake the Best Delicious Easter Cupcakes and Sweet Treats - In Your Kitchen

By Kim Lambert

(Also available in Spanish)

How to Bake the Best Delicious Christmas Cupcakes and Muffins - In Your Kitchen

By Kim Lambert

All Books available from all Amazon sites and other book stores, and available for Kindle too!

HOW TO BAKE THE BEST DELICIOUS FUDGE FOR ALL SEASONS - IN YOUR KITCHEN

Thank You For Buying This Book !

I hope that you enjoy it (and the many delicious fudges that you make).

Image credit :Per Pettersson https://www.flickr.com/photos/per_p/8479806125

Please leave us a review and let us know !

Table of Contents

Acknowledgements xi
Preface xiii
Chapter 1: What is this Book About? 1
   What is Fudge? 1
   What is the History of Fudge? 2
Chapter 2: Tools to Make the Perfect Fudge 5
   Saucepans 6
   A Candy Thermometer 7
   Stirrers 8
   Setting Pans 9
      Lining the Setting Pans 9
      Different Sizes of Setting Pan 10
Chapter 3: Ingredients for Tasty Treats 11
   The Basics 11
      Butter 11
      Sugar 12
      Milk 13
   The Tasty Bits 14
      Nuts 14
      Chocolate 15
      Marshmallows 16

- Locating Missing Ingredients 17
  - Specialty Stores 17
  - Substitutions 18
- Chapter 4: Methodology 19
  - Preparation 20
  - Mixing 20
    - Beating 21
    - Stirring 21
    - Whisking 22
    - Folding 22
  - Soft Ball Stage 23
  - Creating a Creamier Fudge 24
- Chapter 5: Decorating 25
  - Decorating Before the Decorations 26
    - Cutting the Fudge 26
  - Edible Decorations 27
    - Nuts as Decoration 27
    - Complementing Flavors 27
    - Can I use Cake Decorations? 28

More Decorations 29
    Ribbons 29
    Boxes 29
Chapter 6: Recipes 31
    Basic Recipes 31
        Sour cream fudge 31
        Simple Chocolate Fudge 32
        Fabulously Flawless fudge 33
        Microwave Fudge 34
        5 minute fudge 35
    For the Chocoholics 37
        Chocolate Coffee Fudge 37
        Chocolate velvet fudge 38
        Fantasy fudge 39
        Foolproof Dark chocolate fudge 40
        Million Dollar fudge 41
        Rich Chocolate Fudge 42
        Rocky Road Fudge 44
        Triple chocolate fudge 45
        Eat your heart out fudge 46

Easy on the Eyes 49
  Marble Fudge 49
  Layered Mint Fudge 50
  Fudge Meltaways 52
  Ribbon fantasy fudge 54
For the Rest 57
  Buttermilk fudge 57
  Butterscotch fudge 58
  Holiday Fudge 59
  Maple nut fudge 60
  Marshmallow fudge 61
  Old fashioned fudge 62
  Peanut Butter Fudge 64
  Snowy White Fudge 65
  Old time fudge 66
  White Fudge 68
ABOUT THE AUTHORS 70

What Readers are Saying About Other Books in the Series

"I have to say that this book certainly gave me more than I bargained for and it is a bargain. Here you will enjoy not only some great cupcake recipes, but author Kim Lambert takes you back in history to discover how the cupcake came to be called a cupcake, the differences between a cupcake and a muffin, and the original recipe for the first known cupcake. Learn of delicious variations and additives you can bring to an ordinary cupcake, as well as the optimal cooking temperatures, type of pans, and mixing methods for this favorite dessert." - Vickie

"I love cupcakes and muffins! I also love recipes prepared with as much care as a delicious, edible cupcake or muffin. In this book, "How to Bake the Best Delicious Christmas Cupcakes and Muffins" the author has succeeded in winning my highest approval because the details are written in an easy to read, easy to follow manner. I felt the book was prepared with as much love and attention as the recipes themselves. I appreciate the detail, the explanations, the 'what is a...' sections, and most importantly, I appreciate easy to follow recipes. I highly recommend this book." - Jeff

"This is a great little cookbook that is centered on two items, cupcakes and muffins. The recipes are all very clear and easy to understand, with ingredients that you can find at your local grocery store. The layout of the book is visually very appealing and nicely illustrated. The recipes are varied with something for everyone. Also, I think what makes a cookbook great is when crosses all level of cooking skills. This book does this. If you're a new cook, or an experienced one, you will find this book informative. This would be a great book to have when cooking for parties, church events, or just baking at home for the family and friends. Try this book, you won't be disappointed. I have a cookbook collection, but this is one I will go to for cupcakes and muffins." - Barbara270

Acknowledgements

Thanks to all those photographers whose creative commons images have been used, or whose work inspired us to create photos of our own with the same sort of look and feel, or to create and photograph fudge in particular presentations – you are a source of ongoing inspiration.

KIM LAMBERT and CHARLY LEETHAM

Preface

Enjoy Using This Book !

This book is designed to make it easy, and enjoyable, to make delicious, high quality fudge, for any season, and present it in beautiful, decorative and inventive ways, that will make everyone who sees it impressed with your cooking skills, as well as with the fudge that you have made – for its taste, and its appearance.

Image credit Veganbaking.net https://www.flickr.com/photos/vegan-baking/5267223861

Have Fun !

Image credit Alexandra E Rust https://www.flickr.com/photos/aerust/9636353026/in/photostream/

Chapter 1: What is this Book About?

What is Fudge?

Fudge is a soft, confectionery-like sweet. It is served either cold or at room temperature, and is loved at parties, or just for an afternoon snack.

It is usually made with milk and sugar, frequently with chocolate, and can have nuts mixed in for a 'crunch' element.

Fudge can be in many sizes, depending on how many individual pieces you want to produce.

Cutting up the fudge into large squares, for example, won't give you the same amount of servings as smaller squares will.

You can also cut the fudge into decorative shapes, depending on the occasion.

What is the History of Fudge?

The history of fudge appears to have begun under other names, with the components of fudge being very similar to the traditional recipe for 'tablet', which is noted in The Household Book of Lady Grisell Baillie (1692-1733).

The term "fudge" is often used in the United Kingdom for a softer variant of the tablet recipe.

American-style fudge (containing chocolate) appears to be a later invention with one of the first documented mentions of fudge (and a recipe for it) is in a letter written by Emelyn Battersby Hartridge, then a student at Vassar College in Poughkeepsie, New York.

She wrote that a schoolmate's cousin made fudge in Baltimore in 1886 and sold it for 40 cents a pound.

She obtained the recipe, and in 1888, made 30 pounds of it for the Vassar Senior Auction.

As not many cooks had accurate thermometers in the 1880s, it was easy to overcook or undercook fudge.

Therefore, later recipes added corn syrup to prevent crystallization.

Substitutions also included condensed milk, and marshmallow crème instead of the cream, to provide a smoother texture, creating the fudge that we know and love today.

The original fudge recipe reads:

    2 cups granulated white sugar
    1 cup cream
    2 ounces unsweetened chocolate, chopped
    1 tablespoon butter

Combine sugar and cream and cook over moderate heat.

When this becomes very hot, add the chocolate.

Stir constantly.

Cook until mixture makes a soft ball in cold water (234-238°F.)

Remove from heat and add butter.

Cool slightly, then mix until fudge starts to thicken.

Transfer to a buttered tin.

Cut into diamond-shaped pieces before fudge hardens completely.

KIM LAMBERT and CHARLY LEETHAM

Image Credit : m01229 https://www.flickr.com/photos/39908901@N06/8221920773

Chapter 2: Tools to Make the Perfect Fudge

Time and care make good fudge, but first you are going to need some tools to help you prepare the fudge mixture well.

All of these are easy to find, and can usually be located in the cake isle of your local supermarket, or in specialty cooking stores.

The tools that you will need (each discussed in more detail on the following pages) are :

- Saucepans
- A Candy Thermometer
- Stirrers; and
- Setting Pans

Saucepans

To melt down the ingredients, and to boil the mixture to the right temperature, you are going to need some saucepans.

Larger saucepans will be able to hold more ingredients to cook, but smaller saucepans will cook the mixture faster.

Use your best judgment to decide how big a saucepan you need to use for the recipe.

Image Credit : Rev Stan https://www.flickr.com/photos/revstan/3552353896

A Candy Thermometer

One of the essential steps in making fudge is boiling the fudge mixture to a near precise temperature. A thermometer, specifically one for candy, is the best way to find out whether it's time to take the saucepan off the heat.

Fudge needs to be taken off the heat at 116° C / 240° F for the best results.

Candy thermometers can be found in specialty cooking stores, but if you can't get one; there is an alternative! Read on to the Section in Chapter 4, on Methodology, where using the "softball stage", as a measure of temperature and readiness, is discussed.

Image Credit : Neil Conway https://www.flickr.com/photos/neilconway/4656338989

Stirrers

Anything in a saucepan will start to burn, if left sitting there for too long, and fudge is no exception.

Wooden spoons and spatulas will be the best option for slow stirring and thinner mixtures, as you can easily scoop from the bottom of the saucepan to the top.

Image Credit : Alan Levine https://www.flickr.com/photos/cogdog/4420870927

Whisks are better for fast stirring, and for when the fudge starts to harden and you need to break it down some more.

Setting Pans

Fudge will traditionally need at least 2 hours to set properly, and you will need a pan to hold the fudge mixture together until that time is up.

Deep pans have the nice square/rectangle shape that makes fudge pieces much easier to cut, and are easy to fit in the fridge.

Lining the Setting Pans

One of the worst things to happen when baking something delicious is to have it work perfectly... but it's stuck to the bottom of the pan.

There are professional non-stick pans, but these can be difficult to locate for the home cook, and even then they aren't 100% reliable.

The three conventional ways to ensure that your fudge comes out of your pan are baking paper, cooking spray and butter.

Each have their good points and bad points, so it's always a good thing to try one way if another is too difficult, until you find the one that works best for you.

To save time, and to allow you to pour the fudge mixture easily, before the fudge sets too much, line your pan before starting the boiling of the mixture.

Different Sizes of Setting Pan

The recipes in this book will call for pans of many different shapes and sizes, but, unless you are serving your fudge in one giant slab, this is a minor thing – the exact shape is less important than the quantity of fudge mix that will fit into the pan.

Getting the measurements of the pans you're pouring the fudge into is good, as you might just find that your favorite pan can hold the same amount of fudge mix as the size pan you need!

Image Credit : Grannies Kitchen https://www.flickr.com/photos/grannieskitchen/4479504202

Chapter 3: Ingredients for Tasty Treats

As with everything in life, the right mix of ingredients will give you amazing results with your fudge.

Keeping your pantry and fridge well stocked with ingredients will keep your fudge making on a roll!

The Basics

At its core, fudge is made with butter, sugar and milk.

Mixing the right amount of these three ingredients will give you the most basic of fudge, although it won't be very tasty.

Butter

Butter comes in two main types: salted and unsalted.

The only difference is, as you might expect, the percentage of salt mixed through the butter.

In the amount of butter for the recipes in this book, the difference in salt content is less than a pinch. This means that using one or the other doesn't make much difference to the taste of your result.

Image credit : Jessica Merz   https://www.flickr.com/photos/jessicafm/71922825

Sugar

Sugar can be bought in 5 main types: White sugar, brown sugar, raw sugar, icing sugar, and caster sugar. There are also some darker brown sugars (such as Demerera sugar) that can be used in very rich sweets. These types can vary considerably, so is best to use the sugar that is mentioned in the specific recipe.

Image credit : Melissa Wiese   https://www.flickr.com/photos/42dreams/2452033439

Milk

Having the right type of milk is essential for any sweet making, and fudge is no exception.

The difference between full cream and light milk may not be much, but condensed and evaporated milk will change the taste and texture of the result if used incorrectly.

Make sure to double check the recipe before pouring the milk into your mixture!

Image Credit: ~Pawsitive~Candie_N https://www.flickr.com/photos/scjn/3533592997

The Tasty Bits

To make the taste of fudge more interesting, various things can be added, as suits your preference.

Nuts

Having different textures in your mouth with every bite is an excellent sensation, and this is why nuts are found in most fudge recipes. They provide a delightful crunch to contrast with the smooth fudge.

In this book, the best type of nuts have been selected for each recipe, but, if for allergy or taste decisions mean that you want, or need, to substitute another type of nut into the recipe, you can do so and still produce similar tastes.

Experimentation with different types of nuts is a great way to get different tastes with one recipe!

Chocolate

Chocolate is a favorite treat with the majority of the world's population, so it's no surprise that we have a whole chapter for the most chocolaty fudges that you can make!

Different chocolates have different levels of cocoa content, and do taste very different to one another.

- The most common is milk chocolate, which has around 20% cocoa.

- Dark chocolate is slightly bitter, with 50-70% cocoa (sometimes reaching up to 99% cocoa content!).

- White chocolate is very sugary, with no cocoa content except for the cocoa butter, which gives it its taste.

Cocoa powder is what it sounds like: powdered chocolate.

It can be mixed with water or milk for a nice chocolate beverage, but is very useful with cooking as it makes it much easier to mix in, mainly because you don't have to melt the chocolate to begin with!

Marshmallows

Marshmallows have been promoted as a 'spongy sugar', and that's exactly what they are.

Marshmallows are made up of mostly sugar, whipped to a spongy consistency, and coated with a layer of cornstarch.

Image credit : John Morgan https://www.flickr.com/photos/aidanmorgan/2256639109

Whilst some believe that marshmallows are best eaten, all by themselves, after being roasted over an open fire, the marshmallows used in this book are used to add a light fluffy aspect to the fudge.

Of course, any marshmallows left over are a very tasty (and tempting) treat.

Locating Missing Ingredients

In some countries, you may have trouble locating some ingredients for fudge.

There are some stores that will be of use, once located, and you can substitute some ingredients for easier to find ones.

Specialty Stores

If you are outside North America, you may have some trouble locating corn syrup.

However, in many countries, in most local health food stores, you can find light or white corn syrup as well as healthy snacks.

If you like recipes that use corn syrup, and live where it is hard to get, then stocking up on it is wise.

Local baking stores, specialist cake making and decorating supplies shops, or even candy shops may stock useful ingredients like butterscotch chips and almond bark.

Online research will help a lot for locating those hard to find ingredients.

Substitutions

Some ingredients that are difficult to find can be substituted with other ingredients if necessary.

Semi-sweet chocolate is chocolate that has 50% cocoa content, so dark chocolate is a good substitution when semi-sweet is unable to be found. Dark chocolate can also be substituted in recipes that call for unsweetened chocolate.

Marshmallow crème can be made by placing a large bowl (suitable for high temperatures) over a saucepan half full of boiling water, and stirring the marshmallows in the bowl until they are completely melted. 1 cup (225g) of marshmallow crème is equal to 16 large marshmallows.

Image credit : joe jukes https://www.flickr.com/photos/cupcakes2000/5691071786

Chapter 4: Methodology

Preparing, mixing and pouring sound simple, but if not done correctly can result in a fudge with the texture of breadcrumbs, or cause your fudge to not set at all.

Following the method in each recipe correctly (without taking shortcuts) is important. Here are a few more tips to help your fudge making go smoothly.

Image credit : Didriks https://www.flickr.com/photos/dinnerseries/8477102220

Preparation

Not only do you need to prepare the pan that the fudge needs to be poured into, you need to prepare the ingredients that need to be poured into the fudge.

Weighing out the ingredients before starting the fudge making process is very helpful. Use measuring cups and spoons, found in the cake isle, as common household cups and spoons tend to vary a lot in size, and may result in wrong quantities of ingredients.

If you are using a candy thermometer, make sure that it is calibrated correctly. You do this by boiling water and placing the thermometer 5cm/2inch in the water after it has boiled. Boiling water will measure 100°C /212°F. If your thermometer is not measuring the correct temperature, adjust your measuring of the fudge mixture accordingly.

Mixing

There are many ways to actually mix ingredients together.

Some are good for creating air throughout the mixture (helping the result have a light and fluffy texture), and some are good for breaking down large clumps of mix into smaller clumps.

Beating

Beating is one of the best ways to break down large clumps of mixture that may have started to solidify before completely cooking.

This is good for making sure that the mixture is smooth, and consistent throughout your finished fudge.

However, this will also spill very thin liquid mixtures over the sides of the saucepan, so only use when the mixture has started to solidify.

Stirring

This slow, circular motion is great for when the mixture is liquid, and your aim is to keep the heat rising steadily.

However, stirring with more solidified mixtures will cause the ingredients to not combine properly, creating inconsistencies in the resulting fudge.

Using a spoon or a spatula, this way of mixing will ensure that the fudge mixture won't burn on to the bottom of the saucepan.

Whisking

Whisking is great for a fast combination of the powdery dry ingredients, or for liquids that have gone slightly thick. By moving a whisk rapidly in a slightly circular motion, you can mix quicker than regular stirring, which is useful when a spoon doesn't move as well through the mixture. Just be careful to not whisk too hard and spill your fudge mixture over the side of the saucepan!

Image credit : Raelene Gutierrez https://www.flickr.com/photos/raes_antics/3754847642

Folding

Folding is not quite mixing the ingredients through, but more to make sure the mixture is light enough, or to create a marble effect with the final fudge. Using a spatula, bring the bottom of the mixture around and over the top. This should only be used when the recipe asks for a lighter result.

Soft Ball Stage

Throughout this book, you will notice a step that asks you to 'boil until the soft-ball stage'.

Using a candy thermometer, this will be 116°C/240°F.

This is an essential step in fudge making, but if you don't have a candy thermometer handy, all you need is a small bowl of cold water.

As your fudge is boiling, it will start to thicken. Using your best judgment (or a lot of practice), use a small spoon and scoop some of the fudge mixture out when you think that it is ready to be taken off the heat.

Place a few drops into the cold water, and see what the mixture does.

- If the mixture easily forms a ball in the water, but flattens out when you scoop it up with your fingers, the mixture is done.

- If it does not easily form a soft ball, it needs a little more time cooking.

- If it forms a soft ball and stays that way when taken out of the water, unfortunately the mixture is cooked too much.

This way is a lot of trial and error, but the only way to get better at determining the right time to cool down the mixture is to practice.

Creating a Creamier Fudge

There are two main opinions on what the consistency of fudge should be.

- One is that fudge should be firmer, and is somewhere nearer to the consistency of a crumbly cookie.

- The other is that fudge should be very creamy, so that you can see your teeth marks in it when you bite into it.

The majority of the recipes in this book are part of the first category.

You will need to be fast in pouring the fudge into the pan, as it will turn into the consistency of breadcrumbs if left unattended while cooling.

If you prefer having the second category of fudge, leave some excess milk to the side when you're cooking.

Whether it's the normal, condensed or evaporated milk, having a bit more than the recipe asks will help. Just mix in the milk shortly before you pour the mixture into the pan.

Chapter 5: Decorating

Having fudge that looks really good is half of the enjoyment of eating fudge. Not only is food tasted with your mouth, the taste begins with your eyes.

There are a few different ways to decorate fudge. You can use ingredients already used in the fudge recipe, or you can have treats that complement the taste of the fudge.

You can also have different inedible decorations to frame the fudge, or you can have boxes to store the fudge as well as to make it look pleasing.

Decorating Before the Decorations

Cutting the Fudge

Cutting the fudge is a major part in how the fudge looks in the end, and also how many fudge pieces are actually left over.

Cutting the fudge can be difficult when it has completely set, so it is a good idea to do an outline cut before the fudge has completely set.

You will want to trim the edges of the fudge first, as the edges can curve and go thinner than the rest of the fudge when it is setting in the pan.

Cutting the fudge into 2.5cm/1 inch squares make a large number of servings, and is excellent for parties, picnics, or just small social gatherings.

Cutting it larger will give you a smaller number of servings, but will have each serving of the fudge last more than a bite or two.

If it is for a special occasion, cutting up the fudge in special shapes is an easy but nice gesture.

Cutting heart shapes out of the fudge is excellent for Valentine's Day, and star-shaped fudge is always a hit at children's birthday parties.

Edible Decorations

The best decorations are the ones that you don't have to peel off the food before eating.

Whether the decorations were part of the fudge to begin with, or just a bonus, it will get the attention of everyone.

Nuts as Decoration

Many recipes that have nuts in the ingredients list can be made to look tastier. Simply leave a small handful (a bit less than a 1/4 cup) aside, and after you pour the fudge mixture into the pan to set, sprinkle the remaining nuts over the top. Not only does it show what kinds of nuts are in the fudge, it's good for anyone with a nut allergy to keep an eye out for.

Complementing Flavors

Fresh fruit may not be tasty when added to the fudge mixture at the boiling stage of the recipe, but serving fudge with a rich flavor can be made even tastier by adding a slice of your favorite fruit for a hit of freshness, simply placed on top of the cooled fudge before serving.

Try some combinations, and see what your favorite one is! Slicing the fruit thinly and placing on top of the fudge right before serving is recommended

Can I use Cake Decorations?

Decorations used for cakes, such as icing and sugar pearls, are very common for decorating sweets, however it is not recommended for fudge.

Image Credit: Ruth Hartnup https://www.flickr.com/photos/ruthanddave/9538977426

Fudge and icing have very different textures and tastes, and they clash for the majority of fudges.

More Decorations

Decorating fudge can be just as much fun as making the fudge, and you can show off your own style just with a few simple decorations.

Ribbons

Thin ribbons add a flare of color around the fudge. You can wrap the ribbon around one piece of fudge, or bundle up a few and tie them together with a nice bow.

Ribbons come in varying colors and patterns, so experiment with different ones for each occasion.

Boxes

Boxes are a great way to not only transport your fudge around, but to present the sweet as a thoughtful gift.

Clear boxes show what is in the fudge, and tying a ribbon around the box gives it a nice touch.

Gift boxes can be found in most stores, and can hold a lot of fudge in each one.

Just line the bottom of each layer of fudge to prevent it sticking to the other layers, and to the bottom of the box.

Image credit : rawdonfox https://www.flickr.com/photos/34739556@N04/14731945223

Chapter 6: Recipes

Basic Recipes

Sour Cream Fudge

Ingredients

2 cups white sugar
2 tablespoons white corn syrup
1 cup sour cream
1/2 cup chopped walnuts
1 teaspoon vanilla extract

Method

1. Mix the sugar, corn syrup, butter, and sour cream together until well blended.

2. Cook the mixture over a medium heat, stirring frequently, until it reaches the soft-ball stage.

3. Cool the mixture to room temperature and mix in the walnuts and vanilla extract.

4. Beat the mixture until thick and pour into 20cm/8inch square pan.

5. Chill in the refrigerator for 2 hours.

Simple Chocolate Fudge

Ingredients

2 cups white sugar
2 tablespoons (28g/1oz) butter
1/3 cup white corn syrup
2/3 cup milk
56g/2oz milk chocolate
1 teaspoon vanilla extract

Method

1. Melt all of the ingredients in a heavy saucepan.

2. Cook the mixture, stirring frequently, until it reaches the soft-ball stage.

3. Take the mixture off the heat and beat until slightly thick.

4. Pour the mixture into a 20 cm/8 inch square pan.

5. Chill in the refrigerator for 2 hours.

    Optional: Add your favorite nuts before beating the mixture.

Fabulously Flawless Fudge

Ingredients

225g/8oz milk chocolate

2/3 cup (160ml/5.5fl. oz) sweetened condensed milk

1 teaspoon vanilla extract

Method

1. Melt the chocolate and milk in a large glass bowl over hot water.

2. Add the vanilla extract and mix well.

3. Pour the mixture into a 20x10 cm/8x4 inch pan.

4. Chill in the refrigerator for 2 hours.

    Optional: Add your favorite nuts before mixing in the vanilla extract.

Microwave Fudge

Ingredients

2 cups icing sugar
1/2 cup cocoa
1/4 teaspoon salt
1/4 cup milk
1 tablespoon vanilla extract
1/2 cup (113g/4oz) butter
1 cup chopped nuts

Method

1. In a microwave safe mixing bowl, stir the sugar, cocoa, salt, milk and vanilla extract together, until partially blended - it will be too stiff to blend thoroughly.
2. Put the butter over the top of the mixture, in the center of the dish.
3. Microwave the mixture on high for 2 minutes, or until it is smooth. If all of the butter has not melted in cooking, don't worry. It will completely melt as the mixture is stirred.
4. Mix in the nuts, and mix until the mixture is smooth.
5. Pour the mixture into a lightly buttered 20 cmx10 cm/8x4 inch dish.
6. Chill in the refrigerator for 2 hours.

5 Minute Fudge

Ingredients

2/3 cup evaporated milk
1 2/3 cups white sugar
1 1/2 cups (145g/5oz) diced marshmallows
1 1/2 cups (260g/9oz) semi-sweet chocolate chips
1 teaspoon vanilla extract
1/2 cup chopped pecans or chopped walnuts

Method

1. Combine the milk and sugar in a medium saucepan.
2. Cook the mixture on medium heat, stirring frequently, until the mixture reaches the soft-ball stage.
3. Remove the mixture from the heat and add the chocolate chips, marshmallows, and vanilla extract.
4. Beat the mixture until the marshmallows and chocolate chips have completely melted.
5. Add the nuts into the mixture and combine well.
6. Pour into a 20 cm/8 inch square pan.
7. Chill in the refrigerator for 2 hours.

Image credit : Per Pettersson https://www.flickr.com/photos/per_p/8479806125

For the Chocoholics

Chocolate Coffee Fudge

Ingredients

1 cup packed brown sugar
1/3 cup evaporated milk
2 tablespoons light corn syrup
1 cup (175g/6oz) semisweet chocolate chips
2 teaspoons vanilla extract
1 teaspoon instant coffee granules
1 cup chopped walnuts

Method

1. Combine the sugar, milk, and corn syrup in a heavy saucepan.

2. Cook the mixture, and stir over a medium heat, until the sugar is dissolved.

3. Boil the mixture, stirring frequently, until it reaches the soft-ball stage.

4. Remove the mixture from the heat, and stir in the chocolate chips, vanilla extract, and coffee granules. Continue stirring until the mixture is thick.

5. Stir in the walnuts, and pour the mixture into a 20 cm/8 inch square pan.

6. Chill in the refrigerator for 2 hours.

Chocolate Velvet Fudge

Ingredients

4 1/2 cups white sugar
1 tablespoon corn syrup
1/2 teaspoon salt
365g/13oz evaporated milk
1/2 cup (113g/4oz) butter
460g marshmallows
2 cups (350g/12oz) milk chocolate chips
225g/8oz bar milk chocolate, broken up
2 teaspoons vanilla extract
2 cups chopped walnuts

Method

1. Combine the sugar, corn syrup, and salt in a heavy saucepan. Stir in the milk and butter.

2. Cook the mixture over a medium heat, stirring constantly, until it is well combined, and at the soft-ball stage.

3. Remove the mixture from the heat and stir in the marshmallows, chocolate chips, chocolate, and vanilla extract.

4. Beat the mixture until well combined, and stir in the walnuts.

5. Pour into 30x25 cm / 13x10 inch pan and chill in the refrigerator for 2 hours.

Fantasy Fudge

Ingredients

3 cups white sugar
3/4 cup (170g/6oz) butter
2/3 cup evaporated milk
2 cups (350g/12oz) semi-sweet chocolate chips
195g/7oz marshmallow crème
1 cup chopped nuts
1 tablespoon vanilla extract

Method

1. Combine the sugar, butter, and milk in a large saucepan.

2. Bring the mixture to the boil, stirring constantly. Cook until the mixture is at the soft-ball stage.

3. Remove the mixture from the heat, and stir in the chocolate until melted.

4. Add the marshmallow crème, nuts, and vanilla extract into the mixture and beat until blended.

5. Spread into a 30x20 cm/13x8 inch pan.

6. Chill in the refrigerator for 2 hours.

Foolproof Dark Chocolate Fudge

Ingredients

3 cups (525g/18oz) semi-sweet chocolate chips
1 can (400ml/8fl. oz) sweetened condensed milk
1 cup chopped walnuts
¼ teaspoon salt
1 ½ teaspoon vanilla extract

Method

1. In a heavy saucepan, melt the chocolate chips, milk, and salt over a low heat.

2. Cook the mixture, stirring frequently, until it reaches the soft-ball stage.

3. Remove the mixture from the heat and stir in the nuts and vanilla extract.

4. Spread the mixture evenly into a 20 cm/8 inch square pan.

5. Chill in the refrigerator for 2 hours.

Million Dollar Fudge

Ingredients

400g/13.5oz evaporated milk
4 cups white sugar
2 tablespoons (28g/1oz) butter
¼ teaspoon salt
2 cups (350g/12oz) milk chocolate chips
430g/12oz semi-sweet chocolate, chopped
225g/8oz marshmallow crème
2 1/2 cup chopped nuts
1 teaspoon vanilla extract

Method

1. Combine the milk, sugar, butter, and salt in a medium saucepan and bring to the boil.

2. Cook the mixture, stirring frequently, until it reaches the soft-ball stage.

3. Take the mixture off the heat and mix in the rest of the ingredients.

4. Beat the mixture until it is creamy and pour into a 20 cm/8 inch square pan.

5. Chill in the refrigerator for 2 hours.

Rich Chocolate Fudge

Ingredients

4 cups white sugar
1/2 cup (113g/4oz) butter
340g/12oz evaporated milk
2 cups (350g/12oz) semi-sweet chocolate chips
340g/12oz sweet baking chocolate
195g/7oz marshmallow crème
2 teaspoons vanilla extract

Method

1. In a large saucepan, combine the sugar, butter, and evaporated milk.

2. Cook the mixture over a medium heat, stirring frequently, until it reaches the soft-ball stage.

3. Remove the mixture from the heat, and stir in the chocolate chips and baking chocolate until melted.

4. Stir the marshmallow crème and vanilla into the mixture until well blended.

5. Spread the mixture into a 30x20 cm/13x8 inch pan and chill in the refrigerator for 2 hours.

Image Credit : **Rob Marquardt** https://www.flickr.com/photos/sometoast/3122725749

Rocky Road Fudge

Ingredients

2 tablespoons (28g/1oz) butter
2 cups (350g/12oz) semi-sweet chocolate chips
1 can (400ml/8fl. oz) sweetened condensed milk
2 cups roasted peanuts
300g/10.5oz mini marshmallows

Method

1. In a medium saucepan, melt the chocolate chips with the condensed milk, and butter.

2. Cook the mixture, stirring frequently, until it reaches the soft-ball stage.

3. Remove the mixture from the heat and add the peanuts and marshmallows.

4. Stir the mixture until the marshmallows are just starting to melt.

5. Spread the mixture into a 30x20 cm/13x8 inch pan and chill in the refrigerator for 2 hours.

Triple Chocolate Fudge

Ingredients

4 1/2 cups white sugar
1 teaspoon salt
1/2 cup (113g/4oz) butter
365g/13oz evaporated milk
2 cups (350g/12oz) milk chocolate chips
450g/1 pound semi-sweet chocolate, chopped
250g/9oz milk chocolate, chopped
2 teaspoons vanilla extract
4 cups chopped nuts

Method

1. In a large saucepan, combine the sugar, salt, butter, and milk.

2. Bring the mixture to the boil, stirring constantly.

3. Cook the mixture until it reaches the soft-ball stage.

4. Remove the mixture from the heat and stir in the remaining ingredients.

5. Combine the mixture thoroughly and pour into two 30x20 cm/13x8 inch pans.

6. Chill in the refrigerator for 2 hours.

Eat Your Heart Out Fudge

Ingredients

1 1/2 cups icing sugar
3/4 cup milk
1/4 teaspoon salt
1/2 cup (113g/4oz) butter
2 cups (350g/12oz) milk chocolate chips
3/4 cup crunchy peanut butter
1/2 teaspoon vanilla extract

Method

1. Stir, in a large, microwave safe bowl, the icing sugar, milk, and salt.

2. Add the butter to the mixture and microwave for 1 minute on high.

3. Stir the mixture, then microwave on high for 1 ½ minutes.

4. Stir the mixture, then microwave on high for another 1 ½ minutes, or until bubbling.

5. Quickly add the chocolate chips, peanut butter, and vanilla into the mixture. Stir the mixture until blended.

6. Spoon the mixture into a buttered 20 cm/8 inch square tin and press into an even layer.

7. Chill in the refrigerator for 2 hours.

Image credit : photophnatic   https://www.flickr.com/photos/photophnatic/5628175490

Image credit : **Vegan Feast Catering** https://www.flickr.com/photos/veganfeast/4302302045

Easy on the Eyes

Marble Fudge

Ingredients

2 cups (350g/12oz) semi-sweet chocolate chips
2 cups (350g/12oz) butterscotch chips
1 cup peanut butter
300g/10.5oz mini marshmallows
1 cup chopped peanuts

Method

1. Combine the chocolate, butterscotch, and peanut butter in a large, microwave safe bowl.

2. Microwave the mixture on medium for 5 minutes.

3. Stir the mixture until melted, and then fold in the marshmallows and peanuts. Do not completely combine the mixture; it should have a marbled effect.

4. Spread the mixture into a 30x20 cm/13x8 inch pan and chill in the refrigerator for 2 hours.

Layered Mint Fudge

Ingredients

2 cups (350g/12oz) dark chocolate chips
1 1/2 cups (420g/14oz) sweetened condensed milk
2 teaspoons vanilla extract
1 cup (175g/6oz) white chocolate chips
1 tablespoon peppermint extract
3 drops green food coloring

Method

1. In a heavy saucepan, melt the chocolate chips and 1 cup of the milk over a low heat.

2. Once the mixture is melted, mix in the vanilla extract.

3. Spread half of the mixture into a 20 cm/8 inch square pan.

4. Chill in the refrigerator for 10 minutes, and keep the remaining mixture at room temperature.

5. In a heavy saucepan, melt the white chocolate chips with the rest of the milk.

6. Add peppermint extract and food coloring and mix well

7. Spread the mixture over the chilled layer and chill in the refrigerator for another 10 minutes.

8. Spread the remaining chocolate mixture and chill in the refrigerator for 2 hours.

Fudge Meltaways

Ingredients

First Layer

1/2 cup (113g/4oz) butter
25g/1oz unsweetened chocolate
1/4 cup white sugar
1 teaspoon vanilla extract
1 egg, beaten
2 cups graham cracker crumbs (most butter cookies will work)
1 cup shredded coconut

Second Layer

1/4 cup (55g/2oz) butter
1 tablespoon milk
2 cups icing sugar
1 teaspoon vanilla extract

Third Layer

42g/1.5oz unsweetened chocolate

Method

First Layer

1.   Melt the butter and chocolate in a medium saucepan.

2.   Blend the white sugar, vanilla extract, egg, crumbs, and coconut into the melted mixture. Mix well.

3.   Press the mixture into a 28 cm x 18 cm/11 x 7 inch baking tray and chill in the refrigerator for 10 minutes.

Second Layer

4.   Mix the butter, milk, icing sugar, and vanilla extract.

5.   Spread the mixture over the chilled first layer, and chill in the refrigerator for another 10 minutes.

Third Layer.

6.   Melt chocolate and spread evenly over the chilled second layer.

7.   Chill in the refrigerator for 2 hours.

Ribbon Fantasy Fudge

Ingredients

3 cups white sugar
3/4 cup (165g/6oz) butter
2/3 cup evaporated milk
1 cup (175g/6oz) semi-sweet chocolate chips
195g/7oz marshmallow crème
1 teaspoon vanilla extract
1/2 cup peanut butter

Method

1. Combine the sugar, butter, and milk in a heavy saucepan and bring to the boil, stirring constantly.

2. Continue boiling until the mixture reaches the soft-ball stage.

3. Remove the mixture from the heat, and separate the mixture into two equal parts.

4. Stir the chocolate pieces into one half of the mixture, until melted.

5. Add half of the marshmallow crème and half of the vanilla extract into the chocolate mixture. Beat until well blended.

6. Pour into a 30x20 cm/13x8 inch pan.
7. Combine the rest of the ingredients into the second half of the sugar mixture, and beat until well blended.
8. Spread the mixture over the chocolate layer.
9. Chill in the refrigerator for 2 hours.

Image credit : jules https://www.flickr.com/photos/stone-soup/2426627831

For the Rest

Buttermilk Fudge

Ingredients

1 teaspoon baking soda
1 cup (250ml/8fl. oz) buttermilk
2 cups white sugar
2 tablespoons corn syrup
1/2 cup (113g/4oz) butter
1 cup chopped nuts

Method

1. Blend the baking soda and buttermilk, stirring well.

2. Pour the sugar into a large saucepan and add the buttermilk mixture, corn syrup, and butter.

3. Bring the mixture to a boil, stirring constantly, and cook until the mixture reaches the soft-ball stage.

4. Remove the mixture from the heat, and beat well.

5. Stir the nuts into the mixture and pour into a 20 cm/8 inch square pan.

6. Chill in the refrigerator for 2 hours.

Butterscotch Fudge

Ingredients

2 1/2 cups white sugar
1 1/2 cup brown sugar
1/2 cup (113g/4oz) butter
1/4 teaspoon salt
1/2 cup white corn syrup
1 cup light cream
1/4 teaspoon butterscotch flavoring
1 cup chopped pecans

Method

1. Combine the sugars, butter, salt, corn syrup and cream in a heavy saucepan.

2. Bring the mixture to a boil, stirring constantly, until it reaches the soft-ball stage.

3. Remove the mixture from the stove and add the butterscotch flavoring.

4. Beat the mixture until creamy and add the pecans.

5. Pour the mixture into a 20 cm/8 inch square pan and chill in the refrigerator for 2 hours.

Holiday Fudge

Ingredients

3 cups white sugar
1 cup milk
2 tablespoons (28g/1oz) butter
56g/2oz milk chocolate
1 teaspoon vanilla extract
1/2 cup chopped walnuts
1/2 cup figs, chopped
1/2 cup raisins, chopped

Method

1. Melt the sugar, milk, butter, and chocolate in a medium saucepan, stirring frequently.

2. Cook the mixture until it reaches the soft-ball stage.

3. Remove the mixture from the heat and set in a cool place. Do not disturb for 20 minutes.

4. After the mixture is cool, add the other ingredients and beat until very stiff.

5. Knead the fudge in your hands for 5 minutes and flatten it into 2.5 cm/1 inch thickness.

6. Cut the fudge into cubes and chill in the refrigerator for 2 hours.

Maple Nut Fudge

Ingredients

1 cup maple syrup
1 cup white sugar
1/2 cup thickened cream
1/4 cup (55g/2oz) butter
1/2 cup chopped walnuts
1/2 teaspoon vanilla extract

Method

1. Boil the maple syrup, sugar, cream, and butter in a medium saucepan.

2. Cook the mixture, stirring frequently, until it reaches the soft-ball stage.

3. Take the mixture off the heat, and add the walnuts and vanilla extract.

4. Beat the mixture until blended and pour in a 20 cm/8 inch square pan.

5. Chill in the refrigerator for 2 hours.

Marshmallow Fudge

Ingredients

2 1/4 cups white sugar
3/4 cup (175ml/6fl. oz) evaporated milk
1/4 cup (55g/2oz) butter
1/4 teaspoon salt
1 cup (225g/8oz) marshmallow crème
1 cup (175g/6oz) semi-sweet chocolate chips
1 teaspoon vanilla extract
Chopped nuts (optional)

Method

1. Mix together the sugar, evaporated milk, butter, and salt.

2. Bring the mixture to the boil over a medium heat, stirring constantly.

3. Cook until the mixture reaches the soft-ball stage.

4. Remove the mixture from the heat and mix in the remaining ingredients.

5. Pour the mixture into a 20 cm/8 inch square pan

6. Chill in the refrigerator for 2 hours.

Old Fashioned Fudge

Ingredients

2 cups white sugar
3/4 cup milk
1/3 cup cocoa
2 tablespoons white corn syrup
1/4 teaspoon salt
2 tablespoons (28g/1oz) butter
1 teaspoon vanilla extract
1/2 cup chopped nuts

Method

1. In a medium saucepan, mix the sugar, milk, chocolate, corn syrup, and salt.
2. Cook the mixture over a medium heat until chocolate is melted and sugar is dissolved.
3. Stir constantly, until the mixture reaches the soft-ball stage.
4. Remove the mixture from the heat and add the butter.
5. Cool the mixture until the bottom of the pan is lukewarm.

Image credit : Daniel Hanson https://www.flickr.com/photos/marntzu/6338198559

6. Add the vanilla extract and beat the mixture with a wooden spoon until the fudge is thick and no longer glossy.
7. Stir in the nuts and spread the mixture in a 23x13 cm/9x5 inch pan.
8. Chill in the refrigerator for 2 hours.

Peanut Butter Fudge

Ingredients

2 cups white sugar
1 cup milk
1/4 teaspoon salt
2 tablespoons (28g/1oz) butter
1 teaspoon vanilla extract
3/4 cup of peanut butter

Method

1. Boil the sugar, milk, and salt for 10 minutes.
2. Add the butter into the mixture, and continue boiling the mixture, stirring frequently, until it reaches the soft-ball stage.
3. Remove the mixture from the heat and add the vanilla extract and peanut butter.
4. Beat the mixture until it starts to set (Once it starts to set, it hardens fast!)
5. Pour the mixture quickly into a 20 cm/8 inch square pan and chill in the refrigerator for 2 hours.

Snowy White Fudge

Ingredients

2 cups white sugar
1/2 cup (113g/4oz) butter
140g/5oz evaporated milk
195g/7oz marshmallow crème
1 cup chopped walnuts
1 teaspoon vanilla extract

Method

1. In a heavy saucepan, combine the sugar, butter, and milk.

2. Bring the mixture to the boil over a medium heat, stirring frequently, and cook until it reaches the soft-ball stage.

3. Remove the mixture from the heat and add the marshmallow crème.

4. Stir the mixture until smooth.

5. Add the walnuts and vanilla extract into the mixture and stir well.

6. Pour the mixture into a 20 cm/8 inch square pan and chill in the refrigerator for 2 hours.

Old Time Fudge

Ingredients

2 cups white sugar
3/4 cup milk
50g/2oz unsweetened chocolate
1 teaspoon light corn syrup
2 tablespoons (28g/1oz) butter
1/2 cup chopped nuts
1 teaspoon vanilla extract

Method

1. In a heavy saucepan, combine the sugar, milk, chocolate, and corn syrup.
2. Cook the mixture over a medium heat, stirring constantly, until the sugar dissolves and the mixture comes to the boil.
3. Continue cooking the mixture until it reaches the soft-ball stage.
4. Immediately remove the mixture from the heat and add the butter but do not stir it through.

Image credit : Will Powell https://www.flickr.com/photos/powellizer/80583152

5. Cool the mixture at room temperature for 30 minutes, and then add the nuts and vanilla extract.

6. Beat the mixture vigorously until the fudge becomes thick and just loses its gloss.

7. Spread the mixture into a 23x13 cm/9x5 inch pan and

8. Chill in the refrigerator for 2 hours.

White Fudge

Ingredients

2 cups white sugar
1 cup light cream or evaporated milk
1/2 cup (113g/4oz) butter
1/2 cup flaked coconut
1 teaspoon vanilla extract
225g/8oz almond bark
1 cup (50g/1.75oz) mini marshmallows
1/2 cup chopped walnuts

Method

1. Boil the sugar, cream/milk, and butter in a medium saucepan.

2. Cook the mixture, stirring frequently, until it reaches the soft-ball stage.

3. Remove the mixture from the heat, and add the almond bark and marshmallows. Beat the mixture until it is well combined.

4. Stir in the nuts, coconut, and vanilla into the mixture until well combined.

5. Pour the mixture into a 23 cm/9 inch square pan and chill in the refrigerator for 2 hours.

NOW...
Go and Make
Fabulous Fudge
for YOUR
Festive Table !

ABOUT THE AUTHORS

Kim Lambert is an author, photographer, speaker, freelance writer, business woman and entrepreneur, with a background ranging from Technical Management and Development in the computing field to cooking and sewing as part of a medieval recreation group, and making theatrical costumes.

She writes cookbooks and photography books for fun (as a bit of a change from business books!) and also helps others publish their books (regardless of topic!). She lives near Canberra, Australia, and travels as often as possible.

Charly Leetham's goal is to assist small business owners realize the power of the Internet as a channel to market their organizations in an appropriate and cost-effective manner. She helps solopreneurs and small businesses map their business processes and plan their web presence. Charly has a passion for IT and helping people overcome their technology challenges. She has more than 24 years experience in the IT industry.

As a result of her endeavours over the last four years, Charly has won the MCEI Women in Business Marketing Award 2010, been shortlisted for the Telstra Business Woman of the Year 2011 awards and awarded Best Entrepreneur – Service Businesses - Up to 100 Employees - Computer Services category in the 8th annual Stevie Awards for Women in Business. Charly was also named in to the Top 100 Women in Ecommerce 2011 and is an honoree for Website Development in the Women In Business Golden Mouse awards.

In her spare time Charly enjoys good food, drink and company, and sharing that enjoyment. She writes recipe and seasonal books for fun and hopes that you enjoy using them!

Other Books from Dreamstone Publishing

Dreamstone publishes books in a wide variety of categories – here are some of our other books:-

Get Ranked
- The Art of Search Engine Optimisation and Getting Indexed Fast
(The Website Success Accelerator Teaches....)

By Charly Leetham

Coping With Grief

By Penny Clements

Business Strategy :
12 Steps to Business Sanity
How to Optimize Your Profits and Your Time,
Grow Your Business and Get Your Life Back Too!

By Kim Lambert

From The Inside Out:
Breakthrough Strategies for
Mastering Your Finances:
What YOU Need to Know NOW to Change Your Relationship with Money and Achieve Financial Freedom

By Linda Binns

All Books available from good book stores, and available for ebook readers too!

Be the first to know when our next books are coming out

Be first to get all the news – sign up for our newsletter at

http://www.dreamstonepublishing.com

www.ingramcontent.com/pod-product-compliance
Lightning Source LLC
Chambersburg PA
CBHW071024080526
44587CB00015B/2488